25 Fun Things to Do with YOUR FRIENDS AND FAMILY

Thanks to the creative team:
Editor: Tim Harris
Design: Perfect Bound Ltd

Hungry Tomato®
A division of Lerner Publishing Group, Inc.
241 First Avenue North
Minneapolis, MN 55401 USA

For reading levels and more information, look up
this title at www.lernerbooks.com.

Main body text set in
URW Dock regular.

Library of Congress Cataloging-in-Publication Data

The Cataloging-in-Publication Data for 25 Fun
Things to Do with Friends and Family is on file at
the Library of Congress.
ISBN 978-1-5415-0135-5 (lib. bdg.)
ISBN 978-1-5415-4277-8 (eb pdf)

Manufactured in the United States of America
1-43803-33649-10/1/2018

25 Fun Things to Do with
YOUR FRIENDS
AND FAMILY

PAUL MASON

HUNGRY
TOMATO™

MINNEAPOLIS

CONTENTS

Friends and Family

If you have good friends, doing things with them is a LOT more fun than doing them on your own. Here are a few tips for how good friends behave:

SPEAK AND LISTEN

It is important to listen to your friends, rather than just always saying what you think. Don't worry—if they are a good friend, they will do the same for you.

BE KIND TO EACH OTHER

This sounds obvious, but sometimes friends forget to be kind to one another. They start name-calling, showing off, or bragging. These are all common reasons why friendships end.

BE TRUSTWORTHY

If your friend tells you something they don't want everyone to know, do not rush off and tell someone else. And remember, friends never say bad things about each other to other people.

SOMETIMES, GIVE WAY

Do what your friend wants sometimes, even if it is not your number one choice. Forcing people to do whatever you want to do all the time is not very friendly.

Of course, there is no reason why you can't be friends with your family—so all these tips apply to them too!

1. Play Desert Island Picks

If you were marooned on a desert island, what kinds of things would you want to bring along? Interview your friends and family to learn their answers!

1 **Pick eight songs.** If you are playing this with a friend, decide who is asking the questions and who is answering them.
The "castaway" chooses eight songs that are important to her or him.

2 **Play the songs.** The interviewer plays a bit of each song, then asks the other person why it is important. It might be because it is linked to happy or sad events, or because it reminds them of a person or place.

3 **Choose a book and a luxury.** As well as their eight songs, the castaway is allowed to choose a book and one other comfort to take to the desert island.

2. Tell a Ghost Story

If you're camping (see page 25) or having a sleepover (page 28), nothing beats a good ghost story before bed. You could tell a pre-made ghost story from a library book, or you could make up your own:

1 **Pick a location and characters.** Maybe the story could be set among a group of campers or at a sleepover.

2 **Decide what sort of story it will be.** Is the story going to be funny, scary, or surprising? This will help you decide whether the ghost is friendly, a prankster, or just plain nasty.

3 **Come up with a plot.** Your story needs:
- a *beginning*, which tells people where the story is happening and to whom
- a *middle*, which tells them what happens
- an *end*, which reveals how things turned out eventually.

A good rule for stories is that each thing that happens should be a bit more interesting than what happened before.

3. Hold a Tea Party

Some kids only see relatives on special occasions like holidays or weddings. If that's you, why not organize a tea party with your cousins?

Tea Party
Sunday October 18
3 pm
My house

R.S.V.P.

1 **Pick a date**. Pick a date for your party that gives everyone plenty of warning. About six weeks in advance is usually early enough. Send out invitations with the date, time, and place of the tea party.

2 **Make a guest list**. Once people have replied, you can write out a guest list. Use this to make sure you have enough chairs, plates, cups, etc.

> **TOP TIP**
> R.S.V.P. is short for *respondez s'il vous plait*—French for "please reply." Putting it on invitations asks people to tell you whether they can come or not.

3 **Decide your menu**. A traditional tea party menu would have tea, sandwiches, and little cakes. Add some alternative drinks for people who do not like tea.

4 **Enjoy the party**! Make sure the food is ready before everyone arrives, so that when they get there you can enjoy talking to them instead of preparing.

4. Play Charades

Charades is a great game to play with your friends and relatives. The aim is to tell your teammates the name of a book, movie, play, or TV show without speaking.

1 **Establish teams**. You need two teams of roughly equal numbers. For each player on the opposing team, your team writes the name of a book, play, movie, or TV show on a piece of paper.

ALL YOU NEED:
- Pencil or pen
- Small pieces of paper

2 **Set up the act**. The first player is given a piece of paper by the opposition. She or he holds up fingers to show:

A) how many words there are to guess:

B) which word the player is starting with:

C) how many syllables are in the word:

= three words   = first word   = two syllables

CHARADES SIGNALS

Pulling your ear means "sounds like."

Holding fingers close together without touching shows it is a short word, such as "a."

Pointing at your chest means "I" or "me."

Pointing at someone while touching your nose means they got a word right.

3 **Start acting**. Now start acting the words. How would you act *The Secret Garden*, for example? Would you start with "secret" or "garden?" How will you best represent these words?

5. Go for the Gold

Holding a fitness contest makes for great fun with your friends OR your family. Just be careful about asking Grandma to do the long jump—unless she is a very active grandma!

1 **Pick your events.** First you need to decide on your events. If everyone chooses one event, you should end up with at least one thing each participant enjoys.

SOME POSSIBLE EVENTS:

Running. You could have a sprint race from one place (like the edge of a path) to another (maybe a tree 100 yards away). A longer race could be five times around the park.

Timed shuttle run. Set a starting line. Place one bottle 10 yards away, the next 20 yards away, and the last 30 yards away. On "Go!" the stopwatch starts and the athlete runs to the first cone and touches it, runs back to the start, runs to the second cone and touches it, etc. Once all the cones have been touched and the athlete gets back to the start line, the stopwatch is stopped. The person with the fastest time wins.

Long jump. Set two cones about a yard apart. Spray a line of shaving foam between the two cones. Run up to the line and then jump as far as you can. Measure the distance from the line to where you landed. The longest jump wins. If anyone's foot touches the line, their jump doesn't count.

Plank test. For this, you take turns holding the plank position, face-down with your toes and elbows on the ground and your legs and back in a straight line, for as long as possible. The one who lasts longest wins.

2 Check the ground.
Before you start, walk around the area you will be competing in. Check the ground for deep holes that could trip someone, sharp stones, or—worst of all—dog poop.

3 Decide the order and start competing.
Write down the order of competition. For events where you go one at a time, decide who goes first, second, etc. Keep to that order so that everyone gets the same amount of rest.

Now you are ready for the first event. Good luck!

4 Make up a results table.
Write down the finishing order in each event. Give each person points: 1 for first, 2 for second, etc. At the end, add up the points. The person with the fewest points is the overall winner.

RESULTS	1st	2nd	3rd
Run			
Long jump			
Shuttle run			
Plank test			

Overall:
1st _____
2nd _____
3rd _____

STAY SAFE!
Get permission from an adult to hold your competition and make sure they know what all the events are going to be.

6. Rearrange Your Bedroom

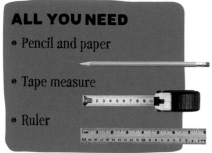

Rearranging your bedroom with your friends is a great way to get new ideas. They might come up with things you would not think of yourself.

1 **Measure and draw a plan of your room**.
First, measure your room from wall to wall. Draw an outline of the room like this:
- For a room 10 feet by 15 feet, you could decide that 1 foot = 1 inch. Use the ruler to draw a 10 in. x 15 in. rectangle.
- Now measure and add the positions of doors, windows, outlets, etc.

2 **Cut out your furniture**. Not your real furniture—just shapes to represent it! For example, measure your bed. If it is 6 ft. x 3 ft., draw a 6 in. x 3 in. rectangle on a new sheet.
Write BED on it and cut out the shape. Do the same for things like chairs, dressers, tables, etc.

3 **Rearrange**. Now you can move the furniture in your room just by moving pieces of paper. Only move the actual furniture once you are happy with your new layout.

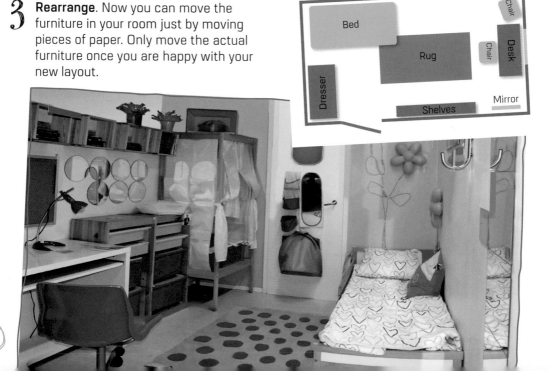

7. Make Oat Bars

If your friends have been helping you redesign your bedroom, maybe you could make them some oat bars to say thanks.

1 **Melt and mix the ingredients**. In a large saucepan, melt the butter, sugar, and syrup. Once it has all melted, stir in the oats—and dried fruit if you want some.

2 **Pour them out**. Line a baking sheet with parchment paper. Pour your mixture into the baking pan and press it down firmly.

3 **Cook and cut**. Put the sheet in the oven for 10 minutes at 350 °F. Take it out and allow it to cool for 10 minutes. Lift the bars out on the paper, put it on a board, and cut into squares.

STAY SAFE!
You definitely need a grown-up with you when making oat bars. Some of the ingredients and equipment get really hot, which could be dangerous.

8. Interview Your Grandparent

ALL YOU NEED
- Pencil or pen
- Lots of paper

You might not know your grandparent as well as you think. These interview questions are guaranteed to reveal at least one thing you didn't already know.

1 Where did you live until you were my age?
Even if they lived in the same town as you, you might not know exactly where. If they moved around, try finding the places on a map.
You might even be able to visit some of them.

2 What was school like?
In your mind, compare their answer with what your school is like. (Tip: don't start telling them about your school. You are interviewing them, so your main job is to listen.)

3 Tell me something surprising about when you were a kid.
Always save your trickiest question until last. This is when you have the best chance of getting a good answer. Your interviewee will have relaxed and gotten used to speaking about himself or herself.

TOP TIP
If your own grandparent is not available, borrow someone else's. Interviewing a borrowed grandparent can be just as interesting and even more surprising.

Draw a Family Tree

A family tree is a chart showing who is related to whom. You will probably need to speak to your parents, aunts, uncles, and grandparents to get all the information you need.

1 Start with you.
Draw yourself (and your sisters and brothers, if you have any) at the bottom of the paper. Add a note saying where you live.

2 Add your parents and grandparents.
Draw a line straight up from your name, leading to your parents' names. Put an equals sign between them: this is the family tree symbol to show that people are married or have children together.

Do the same again with a line leading up from your parents to their parents (your grandparents).

3 Add aunts, uncles, and cousins.
Now draw lines going down from your grandparents to their other children, if they have any. Add their partners and then their children (your cousins).

You may be able to add even more detail than this, with great-grandparents, great-aunts and uncles, etc.

You might need a bigger piece of paper to fit them on, though!

9. Take a "Rembrandt" Portrait Photo

This is a kind of photo named after the famous Dutch artist Rembrandt. The faces of people in Rembrandt's portraits were often lit up like this.

ALL YOU NEED

- Camera
- Key light (light that shines on a person but leaves the background dark)

1 **Position your subject.** The person being photographed will be mainly side-on to the camera, looking toward it. The key light should be shining down on one side of his or her face. The other side will be partly shadowed.

2 **Fine tune the angle.** Now have the person turn their head so that their nose casts a shadow. This shadow should link with the shadow on the side of their face. Just a little triangle of light will be left below their eye.

3 **Take the photo.** Take the photo and check it. Experiment with slightly different positions until you have a perfect Rembrandt-style portrait.

10. Take Great Selfies

Most people know how to take basic selfies. You hold the camera a little above you and look up before pressing the shutter button.

Here are three ways to take more interesting selfies:

1 **Use the timer.** Most cameras and phones have a self-timer button. Using this lets you put more of your surroundings (and fit more of your friends) into the photo.

2 **Use key light.** Key light can give your photos a big impact. Light shining from above, with the person or people in the photo looking upward, can also make for a great photo.

3 **Choose your background.** Think about what is happening behind the person or people in the photo:
- If there is a lot to see in the background, it will distract from the portrait.
- If a person's clothing matches the background color (e.g. a black T-shirt with a dark background behind), the person might blend in and the portrait will not be as good.

11. Go Fishing

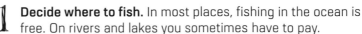

If you have not gone fishing before, see if an older family member could take you. If you already know how to fish, though, you might be able to go with some friends.

ALL YOU NEED

- A fishing rod and reel
- Bait
- Fishhook remover

1. **Decide where to fish.** In most places, fishing in the ocean is free. On rivers and lakes you sometimes have to pay.

   A local fishing shop might tell you good places to fish. They will also know what kind of fish there will be and what sort of bait you need.

2. **Prepare for the day.** As well as your fishing gear, you need to pack a drink and something to eat if you are going to be out for a while.

   Also take warm clothes if it's cold (fishing can involve a lot of sitting around) or a hat and sunscreen if it's hot.

3. **Be patient.** If you don't catch a fish right away, be patient. Spend at least half an hour at the spot you have picked before trying another one.

STAY SAFE

Always make sure a grown-up knows you are going on a fishing expedition and has given permission. Tell them exactly where you will be and what time you will be back.

THROW THE LITTLE ONES BACK

Lots of anglers release all the fish they catch. If you do keep one to eat, make sure it is big enough—there are rules against keeping fish that are too small.

12. Save the Planet before Bedtime

Earth's population is constantly growing, but our planet is not getting any bigger. Each person needs to be more environmentally friendly. Here are four ways to do it:

1 Take a shower. Taking a shower uses significantly less water than taking a bath, so by choosing to shower, you will be using less of Earth's precious water.

2 Walk or bike to school. Earth's temperature is slowly rising, causing destructive storms, melting ice at the poles, and raising sea levels. This is partly caused by the gases released by cars and other vehicles. Walking and biking with your friends do not release these harmful gases.

3 Unplug mobile devices once they are charged. To see why, unplug the charger from the outlet and hold it in your hand. The charger will be warm, which means heat energy is being wasted.

Producing energy releases the same kinds of harmful gases as driving—so by saving energy, you will be helping to save the planet.

4 Go veggie. Crops such as vegetables and beans need less energy and water to produce than meat. You don't need to go completely veggie, but eating less meat will help the planet.

13. Hold a Day of the Dead Festival

On the Day of the Dead, Mexican families gather together to honor those who have died. It is on November 2 each year.

WHAT YOU NEED

- White face paint
- Black face paint
- Black face crayon
- Colored face crayon
- Face paint sponge
- Face paint brush

The Day of the Dead is the final day of a festival that begins on October 31. The festival is a celebration with special food, drinks, costumes, and decorations.

For the festival, people sometimes decorate their faces to look like skulls. As it's a happy festival, they add colors and flower shapes.

1 **Start with a white base.** Use the sponge to put white face paint all over your face except in a big circle around your eyes.

2 **Add black details.** Change colors and fill the eye circles with black face paint. Use the brush to give yourself a black nose and lips, and add a horizontal "stitch" line from each corner of your mouth.

3 **Add flowers.** Add black outlines of flower-petal shapes around your eye "holes." Finally, fill in the petals with bright colors.

Make Champurrado

The Day of the Dead happens when the weather is getting colder. Many people drink champurrado, a thick chocolate drink, to warm themselves.

WHAT YOU NEED

- 4 cups of milk
- 2 cups of water
- 1 thick stick of cinnamon
- ½ cup of Mexican chocolate
- ½ cup of cane sugar
- ½ cup of cornstarch

1 **Warm the milk.** In a medium-size pan, mix the milk with the sugar, cinnamon, and chocolate. Warm it up and let it steam until the sugar and chocolate dissolve. This will take 5–10 minutes.

2 **Make the thickener.** Mix the cornstarch with the water until all the lumps have dissolved. Use a strainer if you need to get rid of any lumps.

3 **Mix carefully.** Add the cornstarch mixture to the pot and stir. Keep the heat low and keep stirring for another 8-10 minutes. Once the drink is like thick gravy, it is ready to serve.

WATCH OUT!

Get a grown-up to help you make *champurrado*. Be careful while serving and drinking it. It will be hotter than you think.

Don't worry, it won't taste like gravy!

14. Play Five Dishes

All you need for this activity is to like eating food. It is a good idea to play this just before mealtime, since you are bound to end up feeling hungry!

1 **Review the rules.** The idea of this game is to pick your five favorite dishes. These are the ones you'd choose if you could only ever eat five different foods again for the rest of your life.

2 **Pick your dishes.** Go around your group of friends, picking one dish each and writing down your choice. Write whether it is a starter, a main course, or a dessert.

　Keep going around until everyone has chosen five dishes.

3 **Make a menu.** Now you all get to agree on a menu. List all the starters and vote for which people like best. Then pick a main course and a dessert.

　Maybe someone will even prepare the meal you have created!

TOP TIP!

Even if desserts or burgers are your absolute favorite, don't pick five of them. You would get bored of eating them in the end.

15. Go on a Shooting Star Expedition

Shooting stars—also called meteors—are not actually stars at all. They are bits of space rock. As they enter Earth's atmosphere they burn brightly before being vaporized.

WHAT YOU NEED
- Blankets
- Tarp (optional)
- Binoculars (optional)

1 **Pick a time.** Shooting stars can only be seen at night. You are most likely to see them during a meteor shower. An internet search for "next meteor shower" should tell you when would be a good time.

2 **Pick a place.** To see shooting stars, you need to be somewhere that the sky is very dark. An ideal place is on a high hill in the countryside. (Always make sure you are allowed on the land.)

3 **Set up.** If the ground is wet, spread the tarp on the ground, then the blankets. Lie back looking up at the sky. It's best to concentrate on one area for a few minutes. Using binoculars might help you to do this.

STAY SAFE!

Stick together so that no one gets lost. Make sure your mom or dad has said it's OK, too, and knows exactly where you are going.

16. Run a Water Balloon Relay

This is a relay race with an added twist—because every player has to get wet to complete the relay. It is particularly fun on a really hot day.

ALL YOU NEED
- Water balloons
- Water

TOP TIP
This is definitely an outside game. For the most fun, run the water balloon relay on a nice, hot summer day with your friends!

1 **Prepare the balloons.** Fill the balloons with water. Make sure there's a bit of space near the opening and you can tie the balloons easily. You need two balloons per person.

2 **Set out the course.** Put half of each team's balloons in a row at the start line and half at the finish line. Make sure it's clear which balloons belong to which team.

3 **Race!** On "GO!" the first player runs out to the balloons, sits on one to pop it, runs back, and sits on another. Only when the second balloon is popped can the next player set off.

    The first team to pop all their balloons wins.

You're going to get wet. Maybe not quite this wet, though.

17. Go Camping for the Weekend

Whether it is with your friends, family, or both, a camping trip is a great way to spend time together. (If you want it to be really different, try making it a digital-free weekend.)

1 Pick a place. The easiest place to hold a camping weekend is at an official campsite. But some families use their backyard or camp in the wild instead. That way they have the space to themselves.

2 Make preparations. There's a well-known saying: "Proper preparation prevents poor performance." When you're going camping, this is definitely true.

Before the weekend, make a checklist of things to take. When you pack, check them off to make sure you have everything.

3 Set up your tent. Putting up your tent in the right place can make a big difference to how well you sleep. Here are a few things to check:
- Is the ground level? You can test this by lying down on it. Try lying in different directions to decide which way your tent should face.
- Are there any sticks or stones there? Move them, or they could damage the floor of your tent (or your back!).

4 Enjoy the weekend! This book should give you lots of ideas for things to do while you are away. You could also look at *25 Fun Things To Do Outdoors* for even more suggestions.

> MY CAMPING WEEKEND: PERSONAL THINGS
> √ Sleeping bag
> √ Pillow
> √ Air mattress
> √ Book to read
> √ Flashlight to read it with
> √ Beanie hat in case cold
> √ Clothes for 3 days (2 days + 1 extra!)
> √ Raincoat/umbrella

GET PERMISSION!

If your group is planning to set up the tents in a field or anywhere that isn't an official campsite, make sure you are allowed to camp there.

18. Play the Five Word Game

The five word game is a storytelling game where each person tells part of a story using only five words. The story can turn out to be funny, spooky, exciting—whatever the players decide. It could start like this:

Player 1   *"The huge wave crashed ashore . . ."*

Player 2   *". . . it raced up the beach . . ."*

Player 3   *". . . there goes the picnic lunch . . ."*

Player 4   *". . . thought Vampire Beatrice as she . . ."*

Player 1   *". . . looked up from the tasty . . ."*
(again)

Here are a few more ideas to get you started:

- The skiers all looked up . . .
- Only one person noticed that . . . .
- *Not again!* thought the *Stegosaurus* . . .
- Even in daylight, a leopard . . .

26

19. Plan a Sleepover

WHAT YOU NEED

- Food and drinks
- Entertainment
- Sleeping bags and pillows (ask your guests to bring their own)

If it is your first sleepover, just invite two or three of your closest friends. Once you have more experience you will feel more confident about inviting more people.

1 **Pick some food.** The ideal food is simple and can be prepared before your guests arrive. Try to pick things you know most people like, instead of just your own favorites.

2 **Decide on entertainment.** You do not need to plan every minute, but it is a good idea to have thought of some games you can all play, a movie you are going to watch, or some other form of entertainment.

3 **Actually sleep.** It is called a sleepover, not an "awakeover"—you all need to go to sleep eventually.

If some people want to sleep sooner, let them. They are your guests, so you should make them feel comfortable.

TOP TIP

Some museums and zoos offer the chance to have a sleepover inside. Imagine waking up among the dinosaurs, or next door to the lions!

20. Make a Flatbread Pizza

If you are having a sleepover, maybe you could make flatbread pizzas. Nearly all kids like pizza, so it would be a popular choice.

1. **Prepare the ingredients.** If you have veggies, make sure they are sliced. If you have meat, make sure the pieces are not too big. Measure out any spices that you will use.

2. **Assemble the pizzas.** Lay out the flatbreads on a baking tray, then use a pastry brush to spread a small amount of olive oil on the tops.
   Sprinkle the flatbreads with the toppings you picked out. Add a bit of grated cheese.

3. **Cook and eat.** Put the pizzas in a hot oven (about 400°F) for 5–7 minutes. Take them out, wait 1 minute for them to cool down, then eat.

WATCH OUT!
Check with a grown-up whether you are allowed to use a sharp knife to cut up the ingredients.

21-25. Five More Things...

You might need help from your parents for some of these activities . . . usually help paying for them!

21 **Ride a rollercoaster**
If you go for a thrilling rollercoaster ride with other people, you will probably all be able to remember it years later. If it was a little scary, you will probably all remember that when it finished you were both relieved and disappointed.

22 **Go to an outdoor movie**
Some warm places have permanent outdoor movie screens. Check in your area to see if there is a theater or park screening a movie outside. Take a blanket, lots of snacks, and something to drink.

23 **Go for a bike ride**
Riding on the road can be a bit dangerous and some parents don't like their kids doing it. Find an off-road biking track and set off on a two-wheeled expedition.

24 **Make a drawing or painting**
It doesn't have to be a pretty country scene. You could draw anything: a building, a car—or just use colors to paint what something feels like to you.

25 **Learn to surf**
Standing up on your first wave is unbelievably fun. Watching your friends falling off as they learn is possibly even more fun.

Index

Picture Credits

(abbreviations: t = top; b = bottom;
m = middle; l = left; r = right)

Shutterstock.com: Africa Studio 1tr/8ml, 29b(6); ag1100 18bl; Allexxandar 23m; autsawin uttisin 10bl; AXpop 14bl; Bacho 19m; Beata Jancsik 30tr; Bragin Alexey 12tl(2); Brent Hofacker 29ml; Chromakey 1tl/6bl; Darrin Baker 17tr; Darrin Henry 28ml; Denys 18ml; Ekaterina Markelova 20br; Ellen Berces 8tr; Estrada Anton 11tl; Everett Historical 14br; Fotoluminate LLC 3/15t; gkrphoto 19br; goodluz 31br; Iakov Filimonov 18br/32tr; IgorGolovniov 14tr; iPics 6t; Jacob Lund 31tl; JIANG HONGYAN 22tr; Juanan Barros Moreno 27bl; Kilroy79 16tr; Kolobrod 12b; Kyselova Inna 29b(3); Leszek Glasner 19tr; leomagdala 29b(2); LeonWang 31tr; Lopolo 10tl; Lyudvig Aristarhovich 22bl; maradon 333 29b(1); mayrum 15mr; michelaubryphoto 1br/22br; Mimadeo 7ml; mkos83 10tr(1); Monkey Business Images 2/11b, 9b, 17b; M. Unal Ozmen 22mr; Nadiia Loboda 13b; Naddya 7tr; n_defender 16tl; Normana Karia 28tl; Nosyrevy 1bl/18tr; Oleksandr Kostiuchenko 12tl(3); Olesia Bilke 1m/25br; Pakhnyushchy 3; Pakhnyushchy 6br; Paul Kulinich 10br; petereleven 8br; Pressmaster 26mr; ProStockStudio 30b; rangizzz 10tr(2); Rawpixel.com 6mr; Ripbinbow 25bl; rock-the-stock 19tl; Roman Mikhailiuk 31bl; Romolo Tavani 27m; Ronnie Chua 28br; Sergiy Kuzmin 29b(4); Siarhei Kasilau 21; sirtravelalot 12ml; Suwat wongkham 3bl/26br; Tiplyashina Evgeniya 24br; Tithi Luadthong 7b; tn-prints 8mr; tugolukof 16bl; Vaclav Volrab 27br; visualgang 8bl; Vitaly Zorkin 12tl(1); Vladislav Noseek 13tl; Volosina 29b(5); Willyam Bradberry 27t; Zivica Kerkez 13mr.

Dan Newman 9ml & mr

THE AUTHOR

Paul Mason is a prolific author of children's books, many award-nominated, on such subjects as how to save the planet, gross things that go wrong with the human body, and the world's craziest inventors. Many include surprising, unbelievable, or just plain disgusting facts. Today, he lives at a secret location on the coast of Europe, where his writing shack usually smells of drying wetsuit (he's a former international swimmer and an enthusiastic surfer).